NURSES
CARE
A WHOLE
FUCKING
LOT
31

NURSE
NEED A
MOTHER
FUCKING
NAP

I'M A SUPER
NURSE
WHAT IS YOUR
FUCKING
SUPERPOWER?

WELL
SHIITAKE

BARNACLES!

DAGNABBIT

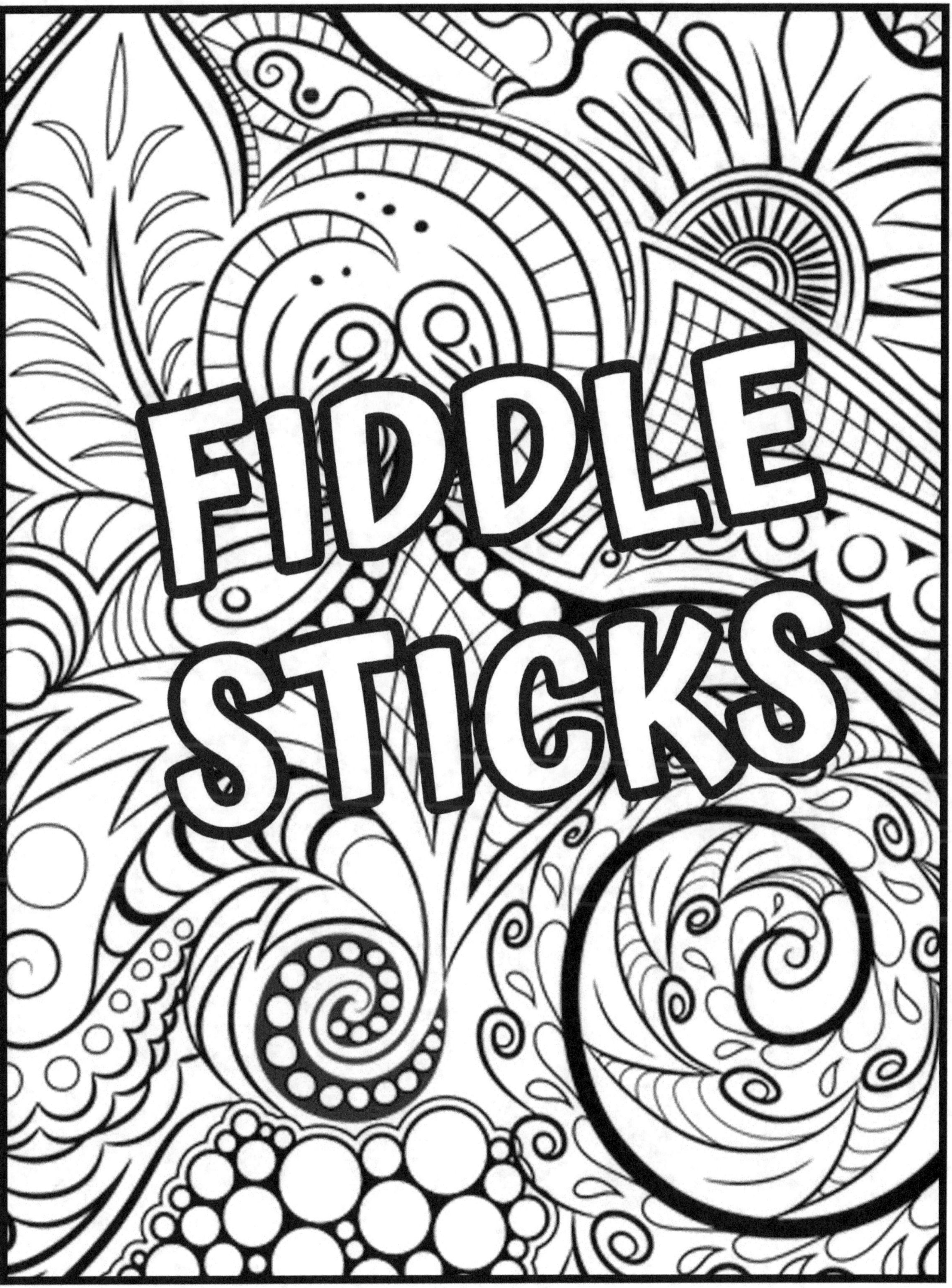
FIDDLE
STICKS

NURSE

BECAUSE FREAKING BADASS
IS NOT AN OFFICIAL JOB TITLE

GEEZ
LOUISE

CRUD

PISHPOSH

OH FUDGE

THUNDERCUNT

YOU MUST BE
MISTAKEN ME
FOR A NURSE
WHO GIVES
A FUCK

HOLY
HAMMERS

MUTHA
FUNCTION

AGATHA
CHRISTIE

SCHNIKES

OH,
MYLANTA!

FUDGE
MUFFIN!

GOLLY!

BARNACLES!

MILF

BULLSHIT

FUDGE
NUGGETS

www.ingramcontent.com/pod-product-compliance
Lightning Source LLC
Chambersburg PA
CBHW081703220526
45466CB00009B/2855